Effortless Style Guide: Perfect Dressing for Any Occasion

Zacharyz X. Rodriguez

<u>Funny helpful tips:</u>

Practice kindness; it's the simplest yet most profound gesture.

Stay proactive in revisiting your reading goals; as you evolve, so might your literary interests and needs.

Effortless Style Guide: Perfect Dressing for Any Occasion : Unlock Your Wardrobe Potential with this Effortless Style Guide to Perfect Dressing for Every Occasion

Life advices:

Rotate between different writing techniques; stream of consciousness, linear narratives, or flashbacks each offer unique storytelling.

Set aside dedicated reading time daily; consistency enhances comprehension and retention.

Introduction

This is a comprehensive resource that provides a wealth of information and practical advice on enhancing your personal style and creating a well-curated wardrobe. Whether you're a fashion novice or someone looking to refine your fashion choices, this guide offers valuable insights to help you navigate the world of men's fashion with confidence.

One of the key aspects covered in this guide is the importance of building the basics of a wardrobe. It emphasizes the significance of investing in timeless and versatile pieces that form the foundation of your style. From tailored suits to classic shirts, well-fitted trousers, and quality shoes, this guide offers recommendations on essential items that should be a part of every man's wardrobe.

Suits play a pivotal role in men's style, and this guide provides insights into different suit styles, fabrics, and colors. It helps you understand the importance of proper measurements and fit, and offers tips on selecting the right accessories to complement your suit, such as ties, pocket squares, and dress shoes.

Shirts are another essential component of a stylish wardrobe, and the guide explores various aspects of shirts, including fabric choices, collar styles, and fit. It provides guidance on different types of shirts, such as dress shirts, casual shirts, and polo shirts, and offers suggestions on how to style them for different occasions.

The guide also delves into the realm of ties, discussing various tie styles, knot techniques, and color coordination. It helps you understand how to choose the right tie length, width, and fabric, and provides insights into pairing ties with different shirt and suit combinations.

Footwear is a crucial element of men's style, and the guide offers advice on selecting appropriate shoes for different occasions. From formal dress shoes to casual sneakers, it covers various types of footwear, materials, colors, and care tips to ensure that you always put your best foot forward.

Understanding how to dress for your body type is another essential aspect covered in this guide. It provides insights into different body types and offers tips on clothing cuts, styles, and patterns that flatter your physique. By understanding your body type, you can make informed fashion choices that enhance your best features.

Shopping for clothes can be overwhelming, but this guide provides valuable tips on the art of shopping. It covers topics such as discovering your personal style, setting a budget, making informed purchase decisions, and maximizing the value of sales and discounts. It also offers insights into online shopping and tailoring services to ensure a seamless and enjoyable shopping experience.

Managing your wardrobe and packing efficiently are essential skills, and this guide provides practical advice on both. It offers tips on organizing your wardrobe, including storage solutions and seasonal rotations. Additionally, it provides a packing checklist and strategies to help you pack smartly and efficiently for different occasions or trips.

In conclusion, this book is a comprehensive resource that covers various aspects of men's fashion and style. From building a versatile wardrobe to understanding body types, shopping smartly, and managing your wardrobe, this guide equips you with the knowledge and tools to elevate your personal style and create a wardrobe that reflects your individuality and fashion sensibility.

Contents

BUILDING THE BASICS OF A WARDROBE

Contrary to the title, this section is not a DIY guide from Ikea, you left that in the top drawer of your kitchen cabinet. Rather this section gives men a guideline for some wardrobe basics that can be combined to make a variety of outfits to suit most occasions.

From bottom to top then:

A couple of quality pairs of shoes, one in black, and one in brown. These will cover most formal and smart casual situations and so it is worth investing in good shoes. It is often said that the first thing a woman looks at when approaching a man is his shoes, so let's get it right from the start!

A selection of legwear:

2 x suits trousers (as part of a suit), in different colours. Generally if you only own two suits then you can't go far wrong with one in navy and one in grey. Choose one in pinstripe and the other in a solid colour.

A pair of chinos, be it in a classic khaki colour, dark blue, or something a bit more adventurous:

2 x pairs of jeans. One for smarter occasions, cut slimmer and in a darker colour, one more casual pair.

A pair of tailored shorts. Yes, there I said it, a pair of shorts. I'll come on to this later in the book, but for now you'll have to believe me!

For your top half:

2 x suit jackets:

A blazer/jacket, in navy, fitted:

4 - 6 shirts. At least one in white, one in light blue. These are the staples.

A couple of quality wool sweaters in different colours.

A selection of polo and T shirts.

A quality overcoat, something like a Chesterfield or pea coat will suit many occasions.

Accessories:

A watch which will suit all occasions. Or if your budget stretches to it, a couple of different ones. A classic metal strapped analogue watch, such as an Omega Seamaster or Rolex Submariner, are popular choice for good reason – they pair with a suit just as well as a pair of shorts and a polo shirt.

A pocket square. If you only own one, then make it a white cotton one, this can give a touch of style to many an outfit.

Plenty of decent underwear and socks.

If you have all of the above then it should give the building blocks of being able to put together a varied, stylish wardrobe. However it is just the beginning, and should be supplemented by each individual's own tastes and circumstances to cater for their own life; after all there is no point in having a drawer full of sweaters if you live on the Equator. What the following chapters cover is the detail of choosing these building blocks of an outfit and how to experiment with mixing items together to create a stylish look for anyone.

SUITS

Many of you will have bought this book hoping to get the edge at work, to be that guy who everyone else considers the stylish one of the office. So what better a place to begin than suits!

Choosing a great suit

When it comes to choosing a suit your budget will take you down one of 3 main routes; off-the-peg, made to measure or full bespoke.

Off the peg is, as the name suggests, a suit made to generic sizes and usually the cheapest of the 3 options. That is not to say that one cannot still spend a great deal of money on an off the peg suit! The suits that you find in high street shops will be off the peg, but so will many of the suits found in more expensive department stores.

Made to measure will be made to order for you from a number of different cut and material choices, but often still in pre-designated sizes and materials, with a limit of varying factors.

Full bespoke is made completely afresh for you, exactly how you like it, designed for your body and finished to your specification. Unsurprisingly this is the most expensive option, but can be well worth it in the long run. Suits tend to take 50+ hours to create from the best tailors found in places like Savile Row. This can mean waiting for over 6 weeks in some cases. But then the best things in life can't be rushed! These top class tailors train their staff extensively and the fit of a bespoke suit will be second to none.

For more about how to choose a tailor for a bespoke suit have a look at the later chapter about shopping.

Recently there has been some blurring of the lines between the 3 types of suit manufacture and one way to get a well-fitting suit without breaking the bank is to buy off the peg and then have adjusted afterwards. Likewise some of the traditional bespoke tailors found in places like Savile Row now do a range of made to measure suits allowing those on a lower budget to access some of the great names in tailoring for less.

So what should one consider when looking for a new suit? Firstly, have a good idea what you want it for and when it will be worn. Wearing it all day in a hot office? You probably won't want a super-heavy wool 3 piece. Likewise it is worth looking to see what others in your workplace are wearing; if you are employed somewhere rather traditional then you don't want to stand out too much with an ultra-modern suit. There is a fine line between standing out for being smart and looking completely out of place at work. When in doubt, play it safe and save the experimenting for social occasions.

To help consider your general options whilst looking for a suit this section is broken down:

Material

Suits tend to be made from a few main materials. Traditionally most suits were made from wool, with more luxurious ones from cashmere. These types on suit tend to hold their shape well and feel soft to the touch.

Today many suits are made from a wool blend, with other materials such as polyester, however these can lead to a rather cheap shiny finish (no thanks!). Blending wool with other natural materials such as cotton or cashmere on the other hand can help create softer or warmer materials whilst still looking sharp.

Lighter suits may be made from linen or brushed cotton. Whilst linen suits are an excellent choice for warmer climates they can be difficult to look after; they crease very easily and can quickly look scruffy if not ironed out regularly. Often linen suits are associated with the 'Man from Delmonte' look – however they are as often made in colours such as medium blue or grey (see example below) as they are in the stereotypical light khaki These alternatives make for great summer office attire or as the basis for a smart-casual outfit.

Suit cloth comes in a huge selection of colours and designs; however the most common are grey, blue and black, either in plain colour, or with a variety of stripes from the thinnest pinstripe to the thick chalk stripe. When having a bespoke suit made the buyer will be able to choose from samples of cloth held by the tailor. As well as the colour, the texture and weave should be considered; each cloth will have a number associated with it, this is the number of threads per square inch. The numbers range from around 150 to 400+. The lower thread counts will tend to feel less luxurious, but will be harder wearing than those with higher counts; it is a trade-off between practicality and the feel of the suit. Predictably, higher counts are usually more expensive.

If you are planning on having two or more suits then it may be worth having a day to day suit in a harder wearing cloth, and a 'best' suit for special occasions or when needing to make an impression made from a finer material.

What colour to go for? Growing up as a kid watching movies about mobsters and secret agents it is easy to come to conclusion that a black suit is the way forward. Generally this cannot be further from the truth. Black suits are difficult to make look good as they tend to drain all but the most olive complexions and the slightest mark or bit of dirt will show up immediately. If you look at stylish men you see in suits either on TV or around your own workplace then they will likely be wearing either a blue or grey suit. The classic colours are a dark navy blue or charcoal grey. These two colours easily combine with most shirt colours to form a smart workplace uniform.

When choosing whether or not to have stripes on your suit, consider what colour you are choosing and how formal you wish to look. Black suits, as previously mentioned, can be rather draining and a bit too monotone in block form, but with a white pinstripe can be brought to life somewhat.   Bold chalk stripe suits, meanwhile, make a strong impression and can be reminiscent of 1980's 'power suits' (think Gordon Gekko), but if pulled off with confidence will have you owning the board room! The safest ground is to go with something like a dark grey or blue suit with a medium pinstripe. The stripe will help accentuate the wearer's body lines, creating a slimming, stylish silhouette.

This simple, single breasted, 2 button navy suit paired with some good shoes is a great example of easy to achieve workplace style.

Some suits also use a checked pattern material, either In something like windowpane check, or even plaid. Due to the nature of a pattern containing squares, it can be difficult to keep a smooth flowing line when wearing such a material and thus isn't advised for the larger man, but can help create an illusion of width for skinny guys. If you are going to choose a check pattern suit then it is best to keep to something fairly subtle such as blue on blue, with the checks being a slightly lighter or darker shade of blue than the rest of the material.

The Cut

There are as many designs of suits as there are materials, but a number of general areas should be considered when thinking about the cut of a suit.

Firstly and most importantly it must create a smooth flowing line over your body, neither too tight nor hanging off you like a bin bag. Suit makers finally seem to be getting this right even at the cheaper end of the market.

Jacket collar hugs shirt collar closely and shoulders fit well

Only top button done up

Good fit around waist

Jacket sleeve slightly too long, doesn't allow shirt cuff to show

Trousers only break once above the shoe showing good length fit

Double or single breasted? This really is a matter of choice and gone are the days when organisations would insist on employees wearing a double breasted suit. There is still a lingering banker image with the double breasted suit, but it is diminishing as more fashion focussed designers have taken this cut on in recent years and made it their own. One thing to remember with a double breasted suit is that it is designed to be worn done up which won't be practical for every job.

Single breasted suits can be cut in a number of ways in their own right, depending on how many buttons are used and the length of the lapels. Generally longer lapels with a less buttons (one or two) create a smarter, more slimming jacket. Three or more buttons with a short lapel can make a suit look boxy.

Suits come 'vented' in three main ways – single, double and un-vented. Rear vents allow jackets practicality when sitting and were originally designed with horse riding in mind. Double breasted jackets being more traditional usually come with double vents.

Italian style jackets meanwhile often forgo the practicality of vents in order to create a more fitted profile.

The previous illustration shows a typical double vented jacket, with one vent at each side.

Meanwhile, this picture demonstrates a single, centrally vented jacket.

Suit lapels come in a number of different styles, but the most common are notched and peak. Notched have, funnily enough, a 'notch' out of the material where the lapel joins the collar part. Below is a good example of a simple notched collar.

Meanwhile, a peaked lapel see the material rise into a peak at the join. Some argue that this draws the eye upwards and creates a slimming effect. The illustration overleaf shows a peaked lapel.

Other suit details

There are a multitude of other smaller factors when looking for suits. A popular topic recently has been that of working cuff buttons. Once all suits cuff buttons worked, but as suits became mass produced this was lost and buttons were simply sown on for show. However real tailors continued to create suits with working buttons. This led to some purposely leaving a button undone, to show off the working function and thus, presumably, let everyone know they were wearing a bespoke suit. Now, however, we have come full circle as some high street brands have caught onto this and have started putting working cuffs back onto some of their cuffs to give the illusion of being higher quality.

Linings are another area to look out for. They are usually made from satin or silk and range from similar colours to the main suit material, to bright, and often outrageous colours. There is no right or wrong here but I am a fan of interesting linings. They are something that nobody needs to see when you are wearing the jacket, but can give a flash of colour when taking the jacket off.

Another thing to consider is the construction of pockets. Some more modern designs use angled or 'slash' pockets to give a sharper look. These are a bit of a double edged sword though and can look a bit too 'trendy' or try hard compared to a flat pocket found on more traditional suit. The below picture shows a good example of some subtly sloping jacket pockets.

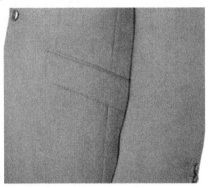

 Also look for pocket flaps - does the suit have them and should you tuck them in? No set rule here - pocket flaps out will give a slightly more casual, yet traditional look, whilst tucked in or no flaps will give a smoother line, adding formality (black tie jackets rarely have flaps) but can look too minimalist on everyday suits. Some suits also have an additional 'ticket pocket' which is a smaller pocket above one of the other waist pockets. This can be a sign of a higher end or bespoke suit, although again this is something that mainstream mass producers have taken on to imitate expensive suits.

Waistcoats

Waist coats can be a great addition to a suit, creating the '3-piece' suit. They are good for both the larger man, helping hold in an unsightly belly, or the slimmer guy, adding any extra layer of material. Waistcoats do tend to bring with them an air of formality, so if your workplace is at the most casual end of business attire then a 3-piece may not be advised. Avoid pocket watches, we aren't in the 19th century and it will make you look too 'try-hard'.

Fashion suits vs Traditional tailors

There is a common misconception that the best suits are those from major fashion brands. Whilst some of these companies have a background in suit tailoring, many do it as part of a much wider clothing line-up. It makes sense therefore that they would be a jack of all trades, master of none? Despite this many men insist on buying designer suits.   The reality is that you will mostly be paying for the label rather than real quality tailoring.   If you want the best suit then go to a proper tailor. You will pay the same amount but will have a company whose sole business is to create the best suits, often based on generations of experience. Not convinced? Just feel the material of the average Italian style (not necessarily Italian brand) designer suit and then compare it to a similar priced tailored suit. Don't get me wrong, the design and cut of Italian suits from their own proper tailors are exceptional, but this does not always translate over to the high-street retail brands.

The above is especially the case for mid-level price suits (£500-1500). Some of the top end fashion houses, however, do create some beautiful suits and often have interesting designs or features that traditional tailors don't, but will have a price to match.   These are a quality alternative to more old-school tailors. Look out for companies such as Zegna, Tom Ford and some of Ralph Laurens higher end sub-labels.

The elements of a well-fitting suit

So now that you have a bit more general knowledge about suits, their materials, designs and construction it is time to examine what actually constitutes a well-fitting suit. There are a surprising number of things that one should look for when trying on a suit, or having one made.

From top to bottom then:

The suit collar should roll around the shirt collar evenly without creasing, and touching the shirt collar the whole way around. Depending on how tall your shirt collar is, it should extrude from the top of suit collar by around 1-2cm.

The shoulder fit is especially important. The edge of the suit shoulder where it joins to the arm must correspond to the same point on the body. Shoulder joint which are down the arm or sitting on top of the shoulder will look very obviously wrong. Too much overhang will make you look like you have borrowed your dad's jacket! If you have a slight frame then avoid jackets with overly constructed (padded) shoulders as this can look disproportional.

The chest fit is best assessed by doing up the middle/top button of a suit. There should only be a very slight X shape created in the material pulling away from the button. Any more than this and it is too tight. If you can pull the suit away from your body when buttoned up more than a few inches then it is too loose. The picture below show's this 'X' and is about as snuggly fitting as one should aim for.

The arm length should be slightly shorter than the shirt arm length in order to allow for 1-2cm of shirt sleeve showing. The suit arm should finish just below the wrist joint. The below illustration shows a jacket which is probably slightly too short, but allows some extra shirt cuff to be shown.

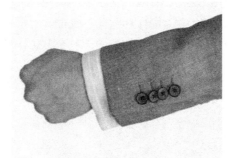

The jacket length should finish just above the top of your bottom.

When it comes to the trousers, the waist should be at the waist (this may sound obvious!) rather than on the hips with a suit.

The trouser leg should break only once at the shoe. The back of the trouser cuff should be just above the joint of the heel and sole of the shoe. This may mean that tailored suit trouser cuffs have a slight horizontal cut to them, raising at the front.

Some very modern style suits may come with shorter than normal leg cuts. This can help achieve the smart single break, but one should be careful not to go too far and end up with a trouser too short where you look like a school boy who has grown out of his clothes!

Suits – finishing the look

You now have the basics of finding and wearing a well fitted suit, but there are a few final adjustments that can make it stand out that bit more. One of the most common and effective is the addition of subtle accessories such as a pocket square.

The polka dot handkerchief above adds a touch of flair without being overly showy or flamboyant. Folding it to a sharp parallel edge rather than puffed up looks more business-like and in keeping with the rest of the look.

Likewise a smart watch will draw the attention of many as much as an out of place, shabby one will. Avoid wearing bulky plastic sports watches with suits, regardless of how expensive they may be.

Instead pair a steel or leather strapped analogue watch; it does not have to be from one of the famous Swiss brands to look smart, there are plenty of low to middle market watches out there which will pair well with a suit. If going for a leather strap try to match its colour to that of your most commonly worn shoe and belt combination; most likely black or brown.

Be cautious when wearing sunglasses with a suit, should you be working outside (because you would never be wearing them inside!). Sports style sunglasses will tend to clash badly with the overall look. Instead look for something a bit more classic such as a pair of aviators or other slim metal framed glasses.

Chapter Quick Summary: Suits

· A Suit's fit is paramount, use the following as a check list of areas to think about:

-     Shoulder fit.

-     Jacket length; should only just cover your bottom.

-     Sleeve length; leave room to show shirt cuff.

-     Fit around the chest/waist; it should slightly pull to create an X from the button.

-     Only ever do up the top button on a 2 button suit, or middle button on a 3 button suit.

-     Collar gap; there shouldn't be one, your jacket should touch your shirt collar and cover ½ of it at the back.

-     Trouser length; look for a single break above the shoe.

-     Trouser rise; suit trousers should sit comfortably above the hips around the waist.

· When considering the options for different types of suits think about the following:

-     Single or double breasted?

- 1, 2 or 3 jacket buttons?
- Off the peg, made to measure or full bespoke?
- Material; wool, linen, cotton, cashmere, blend?
- Colours and patterns; plain, pinstripe, checked, herringbone? Traditional navy, grey or black? Or something more adventurous?
- Pocket angles and working cuffs?
- Linings?
- Slim, wide or standard lapels?
- Notched or peaked lapels?
- What shirts, ties, shoes and cufflinks are you going to pair it with?
- Have you got a good watch to pair with a suit?

SHIRTS

Shirts should be considered as important as a suit when creating a wardrobe for they create a key part of so many different ensembles. This chapter will look first at the main elements of all shirts, what to look for when choosing a shirt and then how to utilise a shirt for different occasions.

As with suits, the key to a good shirt is its fit – neither too tight nor too baggy. To establish whether a shirt is too tight then look at the buttons; if the material between them is stretching away rather than sitting flat, then it is too tight.   Too loose; if it is ballooning at the waist then that is the usual giveaway, although shirts can also look overly baggy if the arms are cut too loose or collar size is too large.

The illustration below is a classic example of a shirt which is too large, both the arms and mid-riff have far too much spare material. It produces a very un-flattering look for even the most athletic builds. The majority of you will doubtless recognise this, either from your own wardrobe or those you work with. It can ruin an otherwise slick look and in particular effects smart casual wear when jackets aren't being worn to hide it.

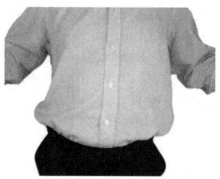

At the other end of the spectrum the following picture shows a shirt which is too tight, demonstrated here aptly by the buttons pulling apart.

You want a shirt to follow the curves of your body without being obstructive or pulling the buttons apart. One way shirts can be fitted but have some 'give' is to have a box pleat on the back which allows some flex.

Many shirt makers now make shirts in a 'fitted' cut, with others calling them 'tailored fit' or even 'muscle fit'.   These are a good option for anyone with an athletic build, although may be too tight around the waist for the larger man.

Most men know their collar size, but don't be afraid to get a shop assistant (or willing other-half) to check every now and again; after all we don't all stay the same size for our whole lives. When buttoned up a collar should be tight enough that you can get no more than a couple of fingers under the collar. A loose fitting collar looks sloppy and can give the illusion of having a skinny neck.

To measure whether a sleeve is the correct length, stand straight with your arms hanging down. The cuff should finish between your wrist and first thumb knuckle/thumb web. If you have a jacket with you then try that one with it. Ideally you want 1-2cm of cuff showing.

The length of the shirt should be long enough to not un-tuck itself when sitting down. Only buy a short shirt if you are planning on wearing it un-tucked – although there are not many occasions when this will be appropriate with a shirt, despite how cool you thought it was when you were at school!

Shirt materials and colours

Most shirts are made from cotton and or linen. Man-made materials like polyester should be avoided like the plague. The exception to this is Lycra and other elastic materials, which if kept to 3-5% of the overall material (look on the label) will give a slightly stretchy shirt which is able to contour the body better, without looking like it's made of a cheap material.

Cotton shirt material comes in different grades depending on the thread count, usually between 120 and 180, with the highest numbers giving the most luxurious smooth feel. Higher grades tends to be more expensive, but ironically can also wear out the fastest.

The way the cloth is weaved into shirt material is very varied today. Most are in what is known as 'plain weave' which gives a smooth look or oxford weave which looks more textured. Other more interesting weaves include twill which can give herringbone type patterns within the material.

The ease of production of shirt material today means that there are tens of thousands of different colour, stripe, check and weave combinations out there. If you visit a bespoke shirt maker they will have books of sample shirt materials to choose from which give the customer a dangerous amount of choice; I remember spending at least half an hour comparing about 10 very slightly different samples of blue stripes, all of which would have made a perfectly good shirt, before choosing one! So make sure you have plenty of time before setting out on a bespoke shirt buying endeavour!

People often ask me when a striped/checked/other shirt should be worn. There isn't a rule here – it really is up to you! However, my personal feeling is that checks should be reserved for more casual occasions rather than worn with suits, although plenty will disagree with this. Plain shirts and vertical stripes will lead to a much smoother look when worn with a suit and draw the eye up-down creating a slimming silhouette. It also depends on what tie you will/won't be wearing; too many lines going in too many directions will create a fussy, busy image, but more on ties later. That being said, a patterned shirt, when worn with solid coloured trouser/jacket can be very eye catching when worn in a smart casual manner (i.e. not at work!), so if you are looking to spice up your wardrobe a bit for evenings out then check out floral or abstract prints. These kinds of things work best in 2 tone; for example a white shirt with a coloured pattern. More than 2 colours and it's going to be getting a bit crazy!

Shirt Collars

Choosing the right collar for a shirt can make a big difference to its look.

The regular collar is the most common and multi-purpose. It looks as good done up with a tie as it does open, worn pared with jeans for a casual look. As such if you are only going to buy a few shirts then at least a couple should have collars like this. One thing to look out for with collars like this is to check how they lie both open and closed; if they are cut too short compared to the height of the collar then they won't look right. Likewise if they are too long then they will have a habit of lying on the shoulder and naturally spreading. You want them to just touch the shoulder ideally.

The spread or wide collar is a particularly formal collar and should only be worn on a shirt which is going to be done up with a tie. Due to the gap created, it is best paired with a fairly thick material tie and/or done up with a Windsor knot. When worn correctly this type of collar looks very smart and add some real style to a suit.

The button-down collar has fallen out of vogue with business wear and is generally associated with more casual shirts now. By their very design button down collars are normally paired with shirts which have softer collars and thus it is difficult to create a sharp look with such a collar.

The height of the neck part of the collar varies from shirt to shirt too. Italian shirts tend to have taller collars and often have two, or even three, buttons at the collar. If the shirt is made of a solid enough material (double thickness collars) or is starched then it will sit up, even when open and can look great. If it is a soft material however, then it will fall open and look sloppy.

The above picture shows a good example of a double buttoned collar, in a tall Italian style. Notice also the contrast inside collar colour with the darker blue. Little details like this can give a shirt that extra edge of style over normal, boring shirts.

Normal and spread collars will often have collar stiffeners – these are removable pieces of plastic or metal which slide into the collar to keep it rigid. Any good quality shirt should come with these so look out for them when purchasing. Make sure you take them out when washing a shirt otherwise the laundry monster will claim them for all of time!

The golden rules of how many shirt buttons to do up:

- Done all the way up only when wearing a tie. Recently there has been a growing fashion of doing up shirts and polos when not wearing a tie. Give it a few months/years and this will no doubt die out again. If you insist on following trends then by all means go ahead and do this now, but don't expect to be classically stylish wearing a shirt in this manner.
- Semi-formal business wear – wearing a shirt and jacket without a tie; undo the top button only.
- Casual when out; undo top two buttons.
- 3 or more buttons undone will not make you look like a playboy, despite what you might think. Don't do it.

Shirt Cuffs

Shirt cuffs come in three common varieties, the double (French) cuff, single cuff and barrel cuff.

The double cuff is most used with formal shirts but this does not mean that it cannot be worn casually. Pared with a blazer and an interesting set of cufflinks can add a nice touch of style. Likewise there is nothing wrong with rolling up a double cuffed sleeve. If anything the double cuff should be the default choice when choosing a shirt.

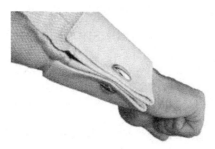

The single cuff is buttoned and has a chink cut out of the corners where the cuff joins to allow freer movement of the hand. Whilst easy and practical, this variation is rather boring and often points to the shirt being cheaper than the usually more expensive double cuff variety.

The barrel cuff is slightly rarer and does away with the chink of the single cuff and adds more buttons to the cuff. This creates some of the formality of the double cuff without the need for cufflinks.

Shirt Pockets

A final piece of advice when choosing a shirt; unless you are planning on putting something in a shirt chest pocket then buy one without pockets. There is no real reason to put a pen in a shirt pocket, it will pull down on the material and quite possibly leak too, so put it elsewhere. A shirt pocket breaks an otherwise smooth look; if you need any further evidence then take a walk down London's

Jermyn Street, the home of British shirt making and try to find a quality shirt with a pocket (you'll struggle).

Chapter Quick Summary: Shirts

· Use the following points as a check-list when considering new shirts:

- Chest fit; there shouldn't be too much spare material around the chest or belly, but buttons shouldn't pull from their holes.

- Sleeve length; cuffs should show below suit cuffs by approximately 1-2cm. Shirt cuff should reach between 1st and 2nd thumb knuckle when arm is held straight.

- Collar type; regular, spread, button down? More formal shirts should have stiffer collars.

- Collar height; regular or high 'Italian' style? How many collar buttons?

- Material and grade; fine or hard wearing? Plain weave, Oxford or herringbone?

- Colours; what suit and tie will it be worn with? Consider stripes and checks.

TIES

So hopefully by now you have an idea what to look for in a suit and a shirt, but what tie to combine with the two? Confused by the massive variation in tie widths? What about patterns and colours?!

First the golden rule of tie proportions: the width of the tie at its widest point should be approximately the same width as the suit lapels at their widest point.

Following the above will always be a good start point and stop you pairing modern skinny lapelled suits with 80's bib ties or vice versa.

Most ties good quality ties are made from silk, some in a smooth printed material whilst others weaved into elaborate patterns, or woven for a textured look. A simple way to test a tie for quality manufacture is to hold it by its short end and let it hang down. It should hang straight; if it twists on itself then it may highlight a substandard tie.

When considering ties with stripes, checks or other designs one must consider what the tie is going to be paired with. As mentioned in the shirt chapter, combining a checked shirt and striped tie can look very busy and untidy. As a rule of thumb it is best to wear relatively plain ties with patterned shirts and vice versa.

Matching tie colours to other pieces of clothing can be a very effective way of subtly highlighting those colours. For example wearing a light blue shirt with a tie of a mixture of yellow/gold and a similar shade of blue to the shirt make the shirt and tie look like they were made for each other. However some colour combinations should be avoided as the colours generally clash, these include: pink shirts and red ties – pink and red tend to combine badly at the best of times, keep away from this combo. Also avoid light pastel shades with bright block colour ties. The contrast in brightness will tend to clash.

Colours that do tend to match well are:

Blue shirts with yellow, gold, other shades of blue, maroon/burgundy (but not bright red). If going for blue on blue then make sure that the tie is a darker shade of blue than the shirt, and never the other way around.

White shirts: almost anything as white is a blank canvas with which to combine anything.

Pink shirts: blue of all shades.

There is no harm in having a number of ties in different shades of the same colour or with differing details. A starter set of ties for any office environment should include: 1 x plain light blue, 1 x solid navy blue, 1 x blue and gold stipe or check, 1 x burgundy (or striped/checked with navy) and 1 x violet/light purple. This will give you one for each day of the week and the ability to mix and match with different shirts easily without too many clashes.

If you are looking for some ties to add some favour to an existing wardrobe then consider textured ties. For example woven ties with a thicker weave. These work well with business suits, but are also a great way to add to a smart casual outfit for a date without looking like you have turned up for an interviews. At the top end of the market Hermes do some very nice woven ties, but they can be found elsewhere for much less.

SHOES

I can't remember the number of times I have seen the advice that good shoes are one of the best investments a man can make. And yet it seems to be one of the most ignored pieces of advice. So here it is once again; buy decent shoes!

First a brief introduction to the shoe and its component parts:

As suggested at the very start of this book, every man should have a couple of pairs of smart shoes which will cover most business wear and smart casual occasions. The most inclusive choice would be to own a pair of black and pair of brown shoes. There are a number of styles in which these can be chosen from, and one pair should be different to the other in order to achieve a better match with a wide range of clothes.

The classic styles of shoes include the Oxford, Derby, full brogue, half brogue, loafers, deck shoes, and various boots such as Chelsea boots. We will go into more detail on the different shoe types shortly, however some of these are more formal than others and of that brief list, probably only the first 3 are really suitable to be worn at work with a suit.

When looking for smart shoes, the smartest will have a lacing system built in to the vamp. This is the case for Oxford style shoes. Meanwhile Derby's tend to have a separate lace piece which sits above the vamp, giving a slightly more casual feel to the shoe. The previous picture showing the parts of the shoe is an example of the latter, Derby style.

The most formal shoes are generally plain leather, although Oxfords are often found with a plain toe cap too. Brogues, a pattern on either the toe area (half brogue) or stretching back over the rest of the shoe (full brogue) are traditionally thought of as being less formal, although today it is perfectly acceptable to wear a brogue with a suit in the office.

Some good examples of classic shoemaking styles for suits and other formal occasions include makers such as Church's.

Kurt Geiger and Bally make some very nice mid-range and higher end shoes respectively. They are on the fashionable side of classic shoe making and as such have a range of shoes that can be combined either with suits or with smart casual wear.

When thinking about shoes to wear with most casual wear such as jeans, avoid highly polished types that were obviously designed for suit wear. Instead think of some of the other materials such as suede, canvas or more matte-type leather finishes. The exception to this are fitted, indigo jeans which can be dressed up; we will speak about this in more detail in later chapters. In terms of design for the more casual outfit, look along the lines of loafers, deck shoes or boots. For very casual jean wear you can combine with trainers (sneakers for those Americans out there!), but make sure they are the fashion type rather than ones designed to actually do sport/running in. The illustration below shows a good example of some relatively plain canvas shoes which can be dressed up or down with different choices of trousers or jeans.

When shopping for shoes there are a few things to look for. When considering more formal shoes, look for a thinner sole, preferably leather. This will look much sleeker when worn with a suit that a pair of clumpy rubber soled shoes. As shoes become less formal the sole can become thicker which will also pair better with things like looser fitting jeans.

There is a difference between highly polished good quality leather and a pair of shoes using plastic-like shiny leather. The former will look smart, the latter will look horrendous. Most good quality shoes don't come out of the box particularly shiny, it takes months of wear and multiple polishes to get the deep, aged shiny finish of a much loved pair.

When buying pointy shoes, you may be able to get away with a size smaller than you would normally wear. This can be a helpful way of avoiding looking like your shoes are too big for you, but make sure that they aren't too narrow and you have some room for manoeuvre at the heel if you are going to do this.

If a shoe brand does half sizes then take the time to try and half size up and down from your normal size. Each manufacturer is slightly different and very few of us are exactly a size 10. Taking the time to do this will pay dividends every time you wear them from that day on.

Casual shoes

When wearing shoes with a casual outfit there is even more scope for different styles. A staple for a smart casual outfit would be to combine something like a chelsea boot, deck shoes or loafers with jeans. This is an easy way to dress the look up or down accordingly - polished boots will look smart, whilst suede or unpolished leather will match a more casual look better.

When thinking about casual and smart casual footwear consider proportions. If you are wearing slim legwear then the shoe can't be too large or your feet will look oversized. For example combining slim jeans with Timberland boots will look very wrong. So either change your legwear or footwear to match each other.

Casual shoes give the wearer an opportunity to add a bit of colour to an outfit too. Burgundy deck shoes can match well with jeans, whilst blue ones work with khaki chinos. When buying such footwear always try to go shopping wearing what you think you might wear them with so that you can see if it works when trying on in the shop.

Chapter Quick Summary: Shoes

· Use the following points as a check-list when considering shoes:

- What are you going to be wearing them with? Make sure your shoe's level of formality matches the rest of your outfit.

- Think about size proportions compared to your trousers. Fitted trousers? Thin soled shoes. Baggy jeans? 'Big' footwear such as boots.

- Think about materials and colours. Offset against what they will be worn with.

- Think about multi-functional shoes that can be dressed up or down with various outfits to suit a number of occasion.

- If wearing smart shoes every day to work then get a couple of different pairs to let them 'rest' and dry out, as well as providing variety to outfits.

TROUSERS AND JEANS

Choosing what to wear on your bottom half can often be a difficult choice. When are jeans appropriate? Will I look like a golfer if I wear chinos out? What about brightly coloured trousers? Worry not, help is at hand.

As with everything we wear, cut and fit is important with trousers, although there are less hard and fast rules about what creates a perfect pair of trousers. When considering a trousers size they are normally labelled as two numbers, for example 32/32. The first is the waist size and the second the length. Waist is just that and should be measured just above the hip. Length is from the inside of the crotch to the ankle cuff.

There are other dimensions to consider too though when looking for trousers; the distance between the bottom of the crotch and the waist band, known as the rise. If this is too long then you will have trousers which sit high and give the 'old-man' look. Likewise if it is too short then you'll end up with a pair of hipsters. Also think about the circumference of the legs, i.e. how baggy the trouser is both at the upper and lower leg.

Jeans

For many a good pair of jeans will be their most worn set of legwear outside of work. Why is it that we so often get it wrong then? Probably because a lot of men assume all jeans are created equal and rarely put the thought into buying them that they deserve. There is as much variety in jean type and just about any of garment out there, so give it the time it deserves.

First some terminology, something there is plenty of in the world of jeans!

Straight cut – These are the classic cut of jeans and as the name suggests are straight throughout the leg with a slight taper towards to ankle.

Boot cut – These jeans flare at the ankle in varying degrees. They often taper at the knee before flaring back out at the ankle.

Wide leg cut – These jeans are made baggier, giving more freedom of movement at the cost of being unshapely.

Skinny or Slim cut – These jeans will hug the wears legs and should be worn with care!

Low rise/High rise – This refers to how the jean will sit on your waist. With high rise being around the waist whilst low rise will sit on the hips (at the extreme known as hipster jeans).

There are also a number of jean 'Washes':

Stone washed – These jeans will be softer than average having been weathered to fade out the colour.

Dirty and Distressed – This wash typically involves being dyed with an additional colour to the normal blue such as brown, giving a manufactured 'dirty' look. Distressing a jean involves either using sandpaper to fray the material or purposely cutting rips into the jean.

Dark or Indigo – This is when a jean is left in its natural state of dark blue. Because they haven't been washed they tend to be more rigid than other types of jeans.

Above we see a Slim Cut Indigo pair of jeans, worn dressed up with some brogues, shirt and jacket.

So, which to wear!?

For a more dressed-up look go for a darker jean without any rips or distressing. The cut should be straight or slightly slim. Baggy jeans should be avoided when worn as part of a smart outfit. For what to pair of dark jeans with have a look at the Smart Casual section.

When buying a pair of smarter jeans there are hundreds of manufacturers out there, each with their own slight twist. Don't be afraid to spend some time trying lots of different makes on when you go on a shopping trip and ensure that you wear what you would normally wear with those jeans so that you can see whether they work in combination with the other items or not. Many jeans that look great on a mannequin may not sit on you correctly or may clash with your shoes or tops.

For jeans that you can wear everyday there is a bit more freedom for individual choice depending on what you are likely to pair them with, but a pair of stone washed lighter jeans in a slightly looser cut will be a safe bet to combine with polo shirts and informal shoes or trainers.

When it comes to looser jeans you must consider what shoes you are going to pair them with. Loose jeans worn as part of a smart outfit with brogues or something similar will drown the shoes and look odd. Loose jeans work best with larger footwear such as boots or fashion trainers rather than slim profile shoes.

Jean fashion changes just like everything else and certain things will cycle in and out of fashion every so often; these include details such as twisted seams which don't run straight down the legs, graphics and stitched patterns, overly low pockets, pockets cut at slashed angles, flaring, dirty look and rips. So by all means go and buy jeans in this category, but be aware that in a year's time they may look out of place when everyone is wearing indigo straight cuts again. If you want to buy jeans that are going to last a long time and stay stylish then keep them simple and well fitted.

Trousers

Trousers in this book are considering pretty much everything that isn't a pair of jeans. Because trousers by default tend to be a smarter option that jeans they tend to be best worn in a more fitted cut. Whilst many of the same general cuts exist as jeans (see above section), the way you should approach buying trousers differs slightly.

Starting with chinos, traditionally they often had pleated fronts, and many still do, but if you want to update the style then find a flat fronted pair. Another 'problem' with chinos of old was that they often had a high rise (the gap between top of the trouser and crotch) lending itself to the old man look. Most high street retailers now cut them much more like jeans, including using jean type pockets with studs and cut horizontally rather than vertically like smarter trousers. This has helped make the chino a much more approachable trouser for casual stylish wear, paired with shirts or polos.

A great thing about chinos is that they come in so many colours. Many will be cautious about adding a pair of bright chinos into their wardrobe, but they can really take your outfits onto another level (in a good way!). Whilst perhaps not for the office, a pair of bright trousers are great paired with a shirt and jacket as an interesting alternative to the jeans that every other man will be wearing in the bar tonight! Be brave, give it a go and you won't look back. (Warning: this sort of thing goes down better in classy cocktail bars than the local pub – know your audience.)

When pairing brightly coloured trousers, your top half should be more restrained to avoid the jester look. Red trousers for example, no longer the reserve of Chelsea types, looks good worn with a light blue shirt and pair of brown brogues. Bright red a bit to bold for you? Try burgundy or maroon instead!

White trousers are another thing altogether though and take some brilliance to pull off, so be careful if considering this look. Keep it to the summer, during the day and in appropriate places (i.e. not at work). Wearing them on a night out will inevitably end up with a glass of red wine down them. Pair them with either bright colours in the blue to green range and a pair of navy deck shoes for the classic Cote D'Azur look, just make sure you actually are on the Med coast and not in Scotland!

If you are not feeling quite brave enough for an adventure into bright trousers then the classic navy blue or khaki chino still has plenty of scope for looking stylish and can be paired with almost any colour.

Try navy blue and a pastel pink shirt with a brown belt and shoes for a timeless look of male elegance.

Khaki chinos are also very adaptable and can be dressed down by being paired with a white T shirt or polo and a pair of deck shoes. Just ensure that if you are going for this look to have a modern style of chino with flat fronts and a fairly slim cut.

Shorts

Right, I did say at the beginning in the 'building the basics of a wardrobe' chapter that a pair of tailored shorts was on the list. When I say tailored in this case it doesn't necessarily mean tailor made, but rather a description of the type of shorts, in other words a pair which are like a shortened pair of trousers rather than baggy cargo or board shorts. A pair made from something like lightweight cotton can be surprisingly stylish when combined with a shirt (sleeves rolled up is a must) or polo shirt, a pair of deck shoes and aviators. It is the perfect attire for the beach or an informal BBQ.

Look for shorts which aren't too baggy so that isn't too much of a disconnect in thickness between them ending and your legs starting (thus avoiding the matchstick legs look) and avoid excess bulk such as cargo pants type pockets. Colours such as navy or khaki are most commonly found and will combine with most colours of shirts without a problem. Ensure they don't go below the knee; ideally they will stop just short of the knee or on it. Too far above the knee and you will end up looking like you've just stepped out of the 50s - beware!

A final word on jeans and trousers

Look in your wallet. No really have a proper look. Do you really need that loyalty card for some place you'll never go to again? Clear it out along with all the other rubbish. Nothing spoils the line of a good pair of trousers like a brick sized wallet. If you are going to take it to the next level then buy a card holder wallet for going out in the evening, putting just the essential cards and some folded notes in there.

Chapter Quick Summary: Trousers

- Use the following points as a check-list when considering legwear.

- Fit; consider all dimensions of the trouser – the length, waist, rise, leg diameter, leg taper and ankle cut. Make sure all compliment your body and type of outfit they will be matched with.

- Consider a variety of fabrics and colours to allow a more dynamic wardrobe rather than just changing your top half to adjust an outfit.

- Think about what you will pair them with, both tops and shoes.

FORMAL WEAR

Most men do not regularly wear Formal Wear, and yet when they do it is often for the most important of occasions; weddings, formal dinners and balls. As with most types of dress, there are many variations on a theme here, although here more than anywhere, there is the distinct possibility of looking out of place with some miss-judged choices.

Black Tie

Choosing a Dinner Jacket

Dinner Jackets, also known as tuxedos after the Tuxedo club in which they were first worn in this manner, come in a variety of styles and colours. The most classic of these is a black jacket and trousers with black satin jacket lapels. The cut even on this 'simple' style fluctuates greatly though and can make the difference between looking average and dashingly handsome. Most men will immediately think of James Bond when black tie is mentioned – but how does the normal guy get to look that good? It's easier than you think!

The golden rule of evening wear is summed up in two words: **Smooth Lines**. If you remember this whilst choosing the various items then you won't go too far wrong.

Dinner jackets, as with suit jackets, must fit correctly. If you are uncertain then have the shop assistant measure you up. Don't be afraid to try on jackets a size up and down from what your official measurement is and see which looks the best. Avoid boxy jackets, and look for something which follows the lines of the body more closely. This creates the effect which I call 'parallel Vs' – this is when the line of body V-ing from shoulder to the waist is parallel to the V created by the lapels of the jacket.

Cheaper diner jackets can often have said boxy look, where the main part of the jacket does not follow the line of the body, but hangs down. Of course the best fitting jackets will be truly bespoke, but this is a very expensive option, especially for something that may only be worn a few times a year. A cheaper alternative is to have an off-the-peg jacket altered once bought – this can make an average priced jacket look twice as good for minimal extra outlay. Having the waist taken in to follow the lines of your body and sleeves taken up to ensure a flash of shirt cuff will ensure that you are wearing the jacket, not the other way around!

Linking into the above idea of parallel Vs is the depth of the lapels and number of buttons on a dinner jacket. Business suits tend to have either 2 or 3 buttons, with either the top or middle being done up when fastened. Dinner jackets however tend to have less buttons; either 1 or 2. This gives a deeper cut and helps create a powerful V shape lending itself to making the wearer looking slimmer. I have seen 3 buttoned dinner jackets occasionally and have to say that I have not seen one person pulling off the look successfully, each time they created a big black boxy bulk of material on the wearer's torso – so my tip for dinner jackets has to be to keep to 1 or 2 button jackets.

When wearing a 2 button jacket, only do up the top button. Generally when stood up it will look smarter to have a dinner jacket fastened up as, again, it will create more of a V shape and pull in the jacket to fit. When sitting down this is often not practical and so it is better to be undone.

There are other things to look for when choosing a dinner jacket. The collars tend to come in one of 3 types, shawl collar, notched or peaked lapel. The shawl collar, displayed opposite, is the most traditional, and to many, the smartest. It gives a smooth, uninterrupted line and personally I'm a big fan of these.

Peaked lapels are more akin to what one may find on a business suit or blazer, but also have benefits; it tends to draw the eye up and outwards with the peak, giving the wearer an extra bit of broadness. However it can disrupt the smooth flow of the jacket.

There is no particular right or wrong when it comes to dinner jacket lapel design; it is much down to individual taste. One area to note though is the material. Generally the lapels are made of satin (see picture above again), this mix of textures offsets the bulk of the jacket well. Dinner jackets with the lapel made from the same material as the jacket, or another matte type material will make the wearer just look like they were wearing a black suit.

Whilst most dinner jackets are single breasted, double breasted ones also exist. Again, this is a matter of personal preference. However it is worth noting that double breasted jackets only really look right when done up, therefore if you are likely to be wearing it to an event where you are constantly going from sat down to stood up then it may become a bit of a pain to be undoing and redoing it up all the time. They can also look a bit boxy at times, that said, I have seen people pull off the look with aplomb and can give slimmer men a fuller look.

Trousers

Dinner jacket trousers will come with the jacket, made from the same material and cut in the style of suit trousers. They usually have a stripe down the leg, also in satin or a similar shiny material. The width of the stripe varies from about 2mm to 2cm. Length of trouser is important when buying a dinner jacket; the trouser should sit on the shoe, only breaking lightly once above the ankle. Any more than this will look too baggy. Remember: Smooth Lines! Formalwear trousers should not have belt loops, nor should a belt ever be worn with black tie. If required then braces should be used instead.

Experimenting with different colours and materials

Formal wear has become more interesting again in recent years, with many outfitters (and wearers) experimenting with different colours and materials. Traditionally midnight blue was often used as an alternative to black (some claiming it actually looked darker than black under certain lights) and this is a trend which has reappeared thanks to some notable wearers such as designer Tom Ford. It is a relatively safe alternative to a black jacket and will have people commenting positively whenever it is worn. I can vouch for this myself!

Other colours that are a bit more daring are deep burgundy reds and very dark greens. Furthermore these colours, as well as black, can be pared with materials such as velvet in a twist on the classic smoking jacket. The important thing to remember with such jackets is that they must still be worn with black trousers, otherwise you will risk looking like Santa's elf! They should also still have the black satin lapel and be cut like a dinner jacket.

White dinner jackets – unless you live somewhere particularly hot, or are trying to look like an extra from an American school prom movie then don't do it. That is all.

Cummerbunds – to wear one or not? Most who wear black tie regularly favour them, they gap the top of the trousers and start of the shirt studs (more on this shortly) nicely, as well as looking smart if the jacket is undone. When wearing a cummerbund it should approximately match the jacket lapels in terms of material; generally they are also made of satin or silk. The pleats should face upwards; there are many theories to the history to this, the most common being that it was to enable a gentleman to slot his theatre ticket into the pleat. Whether this is true or not is beyond me, but either way, that is the correct way to wear a cummerbund.

Another option is a waistcoat. If the latter is chosen then it should be a low-cut waistcoat so as not to ruin the V shape created by the jacket. Unless you are feeling particularly brave then the waistcoat should be kept black or midnight blue.

Dress Shirts

Dress shirts are different from normal business type shirts in a number of areas. They tend to have a double layered front known as the bib area. This is generally a textured area, either with pleats or a flannel type material (AKA Pique' or Marcella, see picture below). Generally the latter is a better choice as it is less fussy than pleats and creates a smoother line. Frilly shirts should be avoided at all costs!

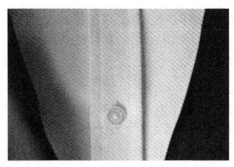

The front of a dress shirt will often have studs instead of buttons. These come in a variety of sizes and materials (silver or gold, inlaid with onyx or mother of pearl are usual) and generally only start about a third of the way up the shirt. This can mean that you end up with a single normal button between the top of your trousers and the start of the studs. This is where a cummerbund comes in useful to bridge the gap. Some studs will be removable for washing, so be careful of this otherwise you may find that you a missing a few after the first wash!

Dress shirt collars tend to come in one of two designs. Normal fold down and wing collar. Normal collars are much like you would find on any other shirt except that they are often also made of the same flannel material as the front of the shirt. Wing collars are much shorter and are more akin to a Chinese collar. Which is to be chosen is generally a matter of personal preference, however traditionalists would say that with black tie it should always be a normal fold down collar, saving wing collars for White Tie (and I would agree). If you decide to wear wings then remember the collar goes under the bow tie, not over it.

Most dress shirts will have a double cuff (also known as a French cuff) and require cufflinks. When there is a choice available always go with a double cuff shirt rather than single button cuffs.

Bow Ties

When wearing black tie one should endeavour to wear a proper bow tie rather than a clip on. It will be obvious to any regular black-tie-wearer which of the two you have on and will set you apart as a black tie pro! Many of you are probably thinking "But I don't know how to do one up" and you probably won't believe me when I say this, but it really is very easy! Ignore the step by step guides online and think of it as a shoe lace. It is the same knot and overthinking it will probably make it more difficult, so just imagine doing up your shoes. Better still don't even look in a mirror until you have tied it, then just use the mirror to adjust to make each side even and straight. Try this a few times and you'll wonder what all the fuss was about!

When choosing a bow tie try it on first in the shop (using the above method) if possible. Some create much larger bows than others, whilst different materials will create either a more rigid or floppy bow.

Generally it is safe to stay with a black tie, hence the name, although shops are always full of colourful variants. For formal dinners it is advisable to stay with black, although midnight blue Is also acceptable. Brightly coloured or patterned bows can ruin an otherwise dashing outfit.

Dress Shoes

Traditionally patent leather shoes are worn with black tie, either in an oxford style or with a more Italian point.   Perforated patent is also not uncommon. However for most wearers it may not be worth spending the amount required for a decent pair of patent shoes for how much they wear black tie in a given year. In this case stick with a pair of black business type shoes, preferably in a plain style such as oxford rather than a brogue, and remember to give them a good polish.

Cufflinks and Pocket squares

Cufflinks when wearing black tie should match the formality of the situation and the outfit in general; it is not the time for 'witty' comedy value links. You cannot go wrong with a pair of plain silver or gold links, although other ideas include ones inset with black stones such as onyx. Understated is the key to black tie and overly 'bling' links should generally be avoided. If choosing between gold or silver then try and match the colour of your watch – i.e. silver/steel watch with silver links.

A plain white pocket square can add a delightful touch to black tie. It should be arranged with a straight edge, sticking out of the pocket by about 1cm. Cotton or silk squares can be used, with cotton working best for this arrangement as it tends to hold shape better.

As ever, think smooth lines and avoid the image of a puffy flower arrangement handkerchief trying to escape from your pocket!

Watches

A good watch will complete the black tie ensemble. Traditional dress watches tend to be very understated and slim in design. They usually have a black leather strap or a very fine-grain metal strap and a plain face. Always analogue and without the multifunction of sports watches, they are simply a way of elegantly telling the time.

Outwear with black tie

When pairing a coat with black tie, aim for a classically styled coat such as a Chesterfield. When buying a coat to wear over black tie (or indeed a business suit), then always try it on when wearing a jacket. Some coats have quite fitted shoulders and make wearing another jacket underneath it almost impossible. You may also find that you need a chest size bigger than you otherwise would to accommodate the extra bulk of a jacket underneath.

It is also traditionally common to wear a shawl scarf with black tie, either in black or white/cream. If wearing a scarf, wear it draped around the neck, rather than worn tied like a regular scarf, and choose a lightweight finely woven shawl of wool, cashmere or silk. Remember once inside to place your outwear in a cloakroom though, continuing to wear your scarf inside is a no-no.

Chapter Quick Summary: Black Tie

Use the following points as a check-list when considering Black Tie.

- The same points for all suits stand here in terms of fit.
- What type of material and colour would you like?
- Shawl or peaked lapels?
- Peaked or normal shirt collars?
- Pique or pleated shirt?

- What cufflinks, pocket square and watch to be combined?
- What shoes? Patent or not?
- Do you need a coat or scarf for the event?

Other Formal Wear

White Tie

White tie is the most formal of evening wear. Generally it is reserved for state dinners and the like, although it has in recent years become more common as an evening wedding dress-state. It consists of long tail coat jacket rather than a normal black-tie jacket, paired with a white/cream low cut waistcoat, white bow tie and wing collared shirt. The trousers are essentially the same as those worn with black tie and the jacket lapels are still in silk or satin.

White tie can be worn outdoors with a scarf/overcoat as per black tie, but traditionally is also worn with a top hat. This is also one of the few occasions that a man can legitimately use a cane! In addition should a gentleman have any medals then miniatures are to be worn.

Morning Dress

Morning dress or 'Tails' was historically a type of riding attire, today it is usually only worn at weddings and certain events such as Royal Ascot. The same general rules of formalwear otherwise apply.

Formalwear Etiquette

Although we live in much more casual days than a century ago, there are still occasions when dress etiquette comes into play. You may be invited to a black or white tie function held by a government or military host for example. If this is the case then it will often be expected that guests know and conform to the dress etiquette of the event. For men this will normally mean that jackets are not removed at all during the evening. The exception to this is when the senior host or guest decides that everyone may remove their jacket due to hot weather or because it has reached a time in the evening when it is acceptable to be less formal. Likewise it is often the case the females will be required to keep their shoulders covered during a meal with a shawl over their dress. If in doubt, ask your host, there is no shame in checking and will be better than embarrassing yourself.

The above probably won't be the case for your mate Dave's wedding. However it is probably worth not being the first to fling your jacket over the dance floor at the wedding reception! You never know, the father of the bride may be a staunch traditionalist.

Chapter Quick Summary: Other Formal Wear

- Use the following points as a check-list when considering formal wear.

- When it comes to White Tie and morning dress, there are plenty of faux pas to be had, make sure you check with an event organiser what they consider to be appropriate.

- You will most likely want to hire this type of wear; this shouldn't mean that you spend any less time making sure something fits properly. If a hire shop won't adjust something for you (many won't for obvious reasons) then try somewhere else to see if they have something which fits you better off the peg before you hire something badly fitting.

OUTWEAR

When the temperature drops it gives us men a whole new layer (if you'll excuse the pun) of possibilities to look stylish. The colder months of the year really are a man's best friend when it comes to looking dashing.

Coats

Most men will have at least a couple of different coats or jackets in their wardrobe and I will admit to having about half a dozen myself. Why? Pairing the right coat or jacket with the rest of your attire will either make or ruin an overall look. However this doesn't mean you have to go out and fill your house with every type of outwear available; there are some key pieces which should cover most eventualities.

The essentials

A smart, classic design coat such as a Chesterfield is a very versatile piece. Essentially a long coat falling between the thigh and knee, single breasted with 3 buttons in a dark colour such as grey or black. This will combine with a suit perfectly, keeping you looking smart whilst out and about on business. An alternative is the double breasted variant commonly known as a Pea coat.

For a second coat/jacket consider something more casual such as a quilted Barber type jacket. This will pair well both dressed up with a pair of trousers and a shirt, or down with a pair of loose jeans and boots for a country-outdoors type look. An alternative could be something like a fine leather jacket which can also be dressed up or down depending on the situation.

There are of course many other types of outwear such as double breasted takes on the classic wool coat, trench coats, wax jackets, gillets, and of course more practical focussed waterproof jackets.

The picture below shows a reversible gillet which of course gives 2 colours for the price of one and so makes it an adaptable item to be paired with a variety of more casual outfits:

Outwear Accessories – gloves and scarves

When wrapping up one shouldn't forget the impact of things such as gloves and scarves, not just on the warmth of your hands and neck, but also in terms of the finishing touches to a great style.

A decent pair of leather gloves is a sound investment and can be picked up for around the £50 mark. Look for ones which aren't too bulky as to make your hands seem disproportionate, but which are still warm. Fine leather gloves lined with cashmere should be able to do style and warmth at the same time without trouble. A quality pair of gloves can be recognised by having well stitched seams with minimal additional material adding to bulk where stitched together. Such a pair of gloves will combine well with a smart coat and suit. If you are really trying to perfect the match then try to get a pair of gloves in the roughly the same colour as your shoes/belt.

Likewise a scarf can add a surprising level of sophistication to an outfit. With a suit ensure that you compliment the smooth look by wearing a finely woven scarf without too much bulk. It should be worn either tied loosely like a tie knot, wrapped around through a single loop once or simply draped around the neck and tucked into a done up coat.

When wearing a scarf with more casual attire then warmer, more bulky scarves can be worn, especially if worn with other bulky items such as thick knit sweaters.

One thing to watch for when wearing fluffy type scarves is that they often mould and can leave other items covered in wool hairs!

Hats

Now, this is a section to approach with caution. Many a man has made a mockery of himself with a misjudged hat! Quite simply some people suit hats better than others and there is no real way around this. So if you are thinking of buying a hat then take along someone trusted to the shops with you and be prepared to walk away with nothing if they say that you look stupid; chances are that they aren't lying!

If you are lucky enough to pull off hats then there are a few things which should be remembered. As with most other items, some hats are more formal than others. Hopefully it is fairly obvious that a baseball cap doesn't go with a suit, but what about the plethora of other styles?

Flat caps are an ideal choice to pair with a more casual outfit. Historically associated with the working class man, they have all but lost this link and are now back as a cool man-about-town accessory. However avoid puffier styles which have been taken over by women and stick to a neater, slimmer cap.

Fedora's meanwhile are a choice for a more formal outfit, combining well with suits. They are brimmed hats with a pinched in crown at the front and usually made of a soft material. Once a common piece of headdress, they are now only worn by the brave and bold, but don't let this put you off. Worn well with a suit will give you an edge of style whilst keeping your head warm and dry.

Hat styles such as the Bowler, Derby and Homberg are all more formal styles again. Bowler hats today are rarely worn except for occasions such as weddings or state ceremonies.

If you decide that you would like to try wearing a hat then there are certain things to remember. Different angles will convey mood more than you might imagine, tilted back to show your face will make you more approachable. Likewise a tilted down brim, shadowing the eyes can look either mysterious, or unfortunately, unwelcoming. Furthermore there is plenty of hat etiquette to conform to: one should not wear a hat indoors, and certainly not to eat a meal. When greeting someone the hat brim should be touched, or if greeting a lady, raised by the crown.

Sunglasses

As mentioned previously in the suit section, one should be careful to match a pair of sunglasses to the rest of the look. Whilst sports style glasses will pair well with casual wear, they do not go with suits or most smart casual outfits. Different shape faces will suit different style glasses, so it is impossible to be overly prescriptive with glasses and sunglasses, but metal frames tend to look more formal than plastic ones. A classic pair of aviators will pair with almost anything.

Chapter Quick Summary: Outwear

· 　　　Use the following points as a check-list when considering outwear.

-　　　What are you going to be wearing it with? Match smart outfits with smart clothes and have casual jackets for every day casual wear.

-　　　Adding a scarf and/or gloves can help add style as well as warmth.

-　　　Hats are another way to add some flair to an outfit, but be aware of what you look like with a hat on!

SMART CASUAL

Smart casual is an area many of us men struggle with; it's the lack of definition which is the problem, is it smart or is it casual? This can be turned to your favour though, look at it as an opportunity to have a bit of creative freedom and stand out!

For the purposes of this book when talking about smart casual, I'm referring to the sort of thing that I'd expect to wear for occasions like a date, after work functions or generally when trying to impress. This isn't a book about dating, but it is a perfect example of when dressing to impress can give a man an edge and so serves us well when talking about what to wear.

So imagine now a first date (sorry married men, you'll just have to go with me on this one or imagine you are meeting your boss and colleagues for drinks). They walk into the room (never be late for a date, it is bad manners!) and see you for the first time in a dressed up way. Immediately you are being judged and in a split second their brain will tell them that you are looking great or not. In your own mind you want to be thinking "I'm looking awesome", doing so will make you smile and give you an air of confidence.

Now dressing for such an occasion is partly a matter of your own taste and circumstances, as with everything else in this book.

However, there are some prescriptive outfits that tend to work well for smart casual. The baseline is the trouser/jeans, shoes, shirt, blazer combo; a pair of dark indigo jeans, cut relatively slim, add a white, light blue or pink shirt, 2 buttons undone, and a navy single button blazer, cut slim. On your feet a pair of dark tan shoes and matching belt. Finish off with a white or navy polka dot pocket square, some silver cufflinks and a dressy watch. Simple as that! The key is to getting all of those ingredients right, based on the advice given in the earlier chapters.

Too hot outside for a blazer? Lose it, but make sure you roll your shirt sleeves up – wearing cufflinks without on jacket will look odd on an evening out. When rolling the sleeves, do a single fold back as far as the cuff (should be about 4 fingers in width), then continue to fold back evenly. This will look smarter than just pushing the sleeve up the arm and will remain in place much better too.

If you want to dress down this image a bit then add a thin wool/cashmere V-neck sweater to the mix. Wearing the sweater will not only keep you warm, but also take the formality out of the shirt.

Wear a V-neck to allow the shirt to open properly – wearing a round neck sweater will often drown the shirt collar or force it shut.

Too cold? Add a thigh length coat, in either single or double breasted style, and combo with a fine-weave scarf. As long as the coat is cut to follow your body lines then it will still look smart and the scarf will give both warmth and style.

Now alter the above by change an item at a time – try some khaki, grey or red chinos instead of the jeans. Switch the navy blazer for a tailored tweed jacket. Try some different shoes (but always shoes, never wear trainers or anything too casual with such outfits). Swap the sweater for a shawl cardigan. Exchange the coat for a quilted jacket. Before you know it you will have 5 or more distinct smart casual ensembles based on a relatively small number of clothes.

A way of adding some smartness to a casual outfit which is often overlooked is adding a tie. Many would dismiss this immediately thinking that ties are the reserve of the office. However, when carefully considered it can really add something to a smart casual outfit. To make the tie more subtle, combine it with a sweater, so that only the first couple of inches of the tie are seen. Pulling this all together with dark jeans and a blazer gives a stylish twist on the normal open necked smart casual uniform.   Ties which work with this kind of outfit tend to be the less formal looking types, for example knitted ties and other coarse textured ties.   Shiny silk ties do not to work as well. Recently very skinny ties were often seen worn with casual outfits. This seems to have been a passing trend though and should not be the default casual tie choice necessarily.

Chapter Quick Summary: Smart Casual

·   Use the following points as a check-list when considering Smart Casual outfits.

-      Have a wardrobe of complimentary items which can be paired up in different combinations to make a number of smart casual outfits.

-      Dress the look up or down by changing single elements such as adding a sweater or changing the shoes.

-      Remember the details such as pairing a decent watch to finalise the look.

CASUAL

This chapter is probably the most difficult to write as casual wear has such a huge scope and tends to be where men really find their individuality. It is also where men are laziest – just because you are dressing down doesn't mean you can't look good! A little bit of thought when dressing casually can turn a man from slob to relaxed gent in no time.

First some rules:

1.   Just because an item of clothing is casual, it doesn't mean it has an endless shelf life. Casual doesn't mean rips, frays and stains; make sure you renew your casual wardrobe as often as smart clothes.

2.   You can't just throw any random selection of casual clothes together and expect to look good – it still requires some fore-thought.

3.   Casual isn't an excuse to wear sportswear - unless you are on your way to the gym or to play a sport!

4.   Casual doesn't have to be boring - you can dress down but still throw in an interesting item of clothing to stand out and give yourself that confidence boost.

5.   Don't mindlessly follow trends. Just because something is currently 'cool' doesn't mean it will look good on you. By all means try, but be prepared to stick to what you know works.

The above is just a start. Casual wear really is a very open field, which depending on your personal style, can encompass pretty much anything. Some of you are probably wondering what your personal style is or thinking that you don't have one. That is fine, this is a good time to create one if you don't have a defined style yet. That doesn't mean you have to throw anyway everything you own and start to only dress like a preppy extra from a Ralph Lauren advert or become an overnight hipster. However it is good to know what you want to look like, then over time craft your wardrobe to reflect that.

So some general tips for making casual wear looks good:

1.   Fit. Yes, there it is again, our old friend fit. Like every other type of clothing, looking good in casual wear will be a lot easier if your clothes fit you properly. Most guys tend to lean towards the too-big side of the spectrum when buying casual clothes. This is understandable as slightly baggy clothes are generally more comfortable, however clothes which fit your body properly will always look better.

2.   Use layering. Adding a few thinner layers can make what you are wearing more interesting as well as practical, compared with fewer thicker layers. It also helps flatter those will less than Adonis-like figures compared with single layers.

3.   Match top and bottom styles. For example, if you are wearing a thick sweater or hoodie then pair that with more rugged jeans or cargo trousers. Remember to think about shoes too; in this case some boots or something similar may work best:

Likewise if you are wearing fitted jeans or chinos then consider tops such as finer knit, fitted sweaters or jackets and sleeker footwear like deck shoes or casual trainers such as these below:

4.   Accessorise, but go easy on it. Add a flash of colour with a bright T shirt or colourful belt. Make sure you don't add too many bold items and minimise 'man jewellery' - stick to a watch. Other options to add a bit of personality include casual hats.

5.   Change where you buy your clothes from. It is too easy to always use the same few shops because you have bought things from there before. Explore and experiment, you may surprise yourself.

6.   Look at what other people are wearing. Women are very good at this, but it is something most men rarely do - check each other out!   You don't have to look at endless mens' magazines to find images of stylish men, just keep your eye out when out and

about. Then try and make a mental note of why that person was looking good, what they were wearing and what they had combined it with. Then feel free to copy them and see if that works for you too. Remember it's often the details which make a difference, so take note of the little things like what belts people wear for example, or how their trousers sit on their shoes - something which subconsciously makes the outfit work, but unless you are looking for that detail probably wouldn't have noticed.

How to dress for your body type

The golden rule to any clothes is to ensure that they have a good fit.

It may seem obvious, but it is the most commonly forgotten piece of advice.   This is especially the case for those who think that they have something to hide. Countless times skinny guys have worn loose clothes, hoping they may add some extra material bulk. This doesn't work guys – it just makes you look like a tent pole with tent flapping around it!   At the other end of the spectrum, bigger men also seem to go for overly loose clothes in the hope that they will flatter, rather than highlight protruding fat. A reasonable idea, but unfortunately also a wrong one; instead this will simply add more bulk and look boxy.

So whether you are slim or large, wear clothes that fit you. Honestly, it will look better!

There are some 'tricks' to flatter your body for those blessed with less than perfect. We'll break it down in this chapter for the most common body types.

Skinny

Layering is your friend. Simply sticking on a massive down jacket isn't going to work I'm afraid. Instead think about adding more layers to what you wear, especially in the colder months. Combine a T shirt under a shirt, then a thin sweater and finally a jacket. This will keep you just as warm as a thick coat and has the added benefit of being more adaptable should you go indoors, enabling to take off as many layers as necessary to keep you warm/cool. But the real beauty is that if each layer is well fitting, then they entire ensemble will follow the natural lines of your body, but give you some extra inches of width.

A jacket that I have seen work well with the skinnier type is a quilted Barbour type jacket with side tabs which allow the waist to be adjusted. These jackets, if bought in the right size will follow your body line and give a bit of extra bulk without looking ridiculous. Furthermore they combine well with both casual and smart casual to give your wardrobe some real flexibility.

This is less easy with trousers, but again, rather than going for overly baggy trousers to hide your pin legs, wear something with a regular to slim fit, straight leg cut.

Large and Heavy Set

As alluded to in the introduction to this chapter, the bigger man should avoid wearing overly loose clothes to try to hide unruly curves. Instead, wear clothes that draw the eye away from those areas or create an optical illusion of sorts.   The most common way to do this is to incorporate stripes into your wardrobe. Vertical stripes work well, especially with business and smart casual wear, but so do horizontal stripes, contrary to popular belief.   A pin or chalk stripe suit will draw the eye up and down the body, giving the impression of a slimmer, taller silhouette. Meanwhile, avoid busy patterns, especially repetitive ones.

Avoid trousers with pleats. These are becoming less common anyway, but there is an old myth that pleats will help flatter the bigger guy. Quite the opposite is true.

Bigger guys should tend towards V neck rather than round neck T shirts and sweaters; this will give the illusion of a longer, slimmer neck and break up the bulk of your upper body. Other clothing tricks to draw the eye away are things such as shoulder epaulettes on jackets and flashes of colour using bright layering.

When wearing a belt, make sure you buy one with ample extra length. Being on the last belt hole and still straining will only draw the eye of others to that area. Buy a new, longer belt, and have it done up comfortably rather than over-tight.

When appropriate, wear a tie, it will draw the eye up and down and take emphasis off any bulk.

For suits, avoid double vented jackets as the square that these create at the bottom of the jacket emphasise any size. Instead opt for a single, central vented jacket.

Short Men

If you are of a shorter stature, the first thing to remember is to stand up straight! Most people tend to slouch a bit; you can get away with this if you are 6'4", but not if you are 5'4"! Imagine a string coming from the top of your head pulling you upwards and pull your shoulders back a bit. That will probably give you an extra inch straight away.

When it comes to clothes for shorter men it is all about creating the illusion of height through the use of proportions. You should simply look like a tall guy who is further away! So once again, make sure clothes fit well and avoid things which drown your body. Dressing in slightly more snuggly fitting clothes will keep the proportions of your body in place. Avoid things like pointy shoes as they will look oversized. Consider wearing vertical stripes, be it T-shirts casually, or pinstripe suits for work as they will draw the eye up and down the body.

Give yourself a rise by wearing a slight heel on your shoes. The key here is *slight*; there is nothing cool about a short guy wearing huge Cuban heels to try to make up some height! So avoid clumpy soles, but go for shoes or boots with a natural heel raise.

How to buy clothes – the art of shopping

For most of us buying clothes happens in a number of similar ways - we happen to be walking around a shopping centre with girlfriend, wife or alone and wander into the odd shop, see something vaguely like something we already own and buy it without much thought. Or occasionally we have to go to an event, or new job which forces the purchase of a particular garment, which leads to a similar bit of wandering and then random purchasing.

Seasonal buying

When the seasons change we inevitably find a hole in our wardrobe and have to consider what we need to go with the new trousers that we bought during the last season. It is easy to go about this in a piecemeal way, but makes more sense to think about all the clothes you own collectively. Consider a number of outfits that you might need for a variety of occasions, then think about what you could add to your wardrobe which could be utilised in a number of outfits, thus getting plenty of wears (and thus value for money, see below) from something. The opposite of this is realising that you don't have a sweater which goes with a particular pair of trousers, for example, and buying something which only goes with that but nothing else, leading to a wardrobe full of individual items which only work with one of two other things, rather than being flexible.

Cost vs Cost-per-wear

Something that many people (men and women alike!) don't consider when buying clothes is cost-per-wear. This is an easy way of making decisions when considering whether something is too expensive or not. For example, a suit may be a relatively pricey purchase, but if you wear it every other day to work, then over time the cost-per-wear is fairly small, and therefore worth buying. Many of us spend large amounts on things that we almost never wear though. If you are looking at something and thinking "I like this, but

I'm not sure when I'll wear it" or wondering what you will wear it with, then chances are you'll wear it once or twice then confine it to the back of the wardrobe.

Looking at the above, if we take a £500 suit and you wear it 100 times a year (twice a week 50 weeks of the year is a conservative estimate), then after a couple of years it has worked out to be £2.50 a wear. If you buy an unusual £50 sweater, wear it twice then never again then that is £25 a wear. Suddenly all those £20-70 impulse purchases don't look so reasonable after all!

The best time to shop

When shopping you don't want to be fighting the crowds, so avoid peak times by going early in the day or close to closing time (but not so close that you are rushed before they lock you in and buy impulsively). When buying shoes the best time of day is the afternoon as feet tend to swell throughout the day slightly, especially if you have been walking around a lot. Therefore trying shoes on when your feet are at their biggest will ensure that you don't buy too small.

Choosing a suit tailor

When choosing a tailor to make a suit for you there should be a mental checklist of things to go through. First it is important to have a reasonable idea of what you want before going to see a tailor, otherwise it will be all too easy for them to lead you towards something *they* like.

If you have friends or colleagues who have had suits made then ask where they had them done and how their experience of a tailor panned out. The most expensive tailors aren't always the best, whilst some small, relatively obscure tailors can be hidden gems.

Once you have found a tailor you like the sound of then go and see them in person. Ask to see some examples of suits that they have made; they will normally have part finished suits waiting for customers coming for a fitting, or completed ones waiting to be picked up that you can look at.

Next discuss what sort of suit that you are interested in and check that the tailor usually makes that kind of suit. For example if you were you buy on Savile Row in London then most of the tailors there are very traditionally English and so if you were looking for a particularly European cut then it may not be the best place to shop. Likewise Milan isn't going to be the best place to find a British tailor. Whilst most good tailors can turn their hand to other styles, if you are going to go to the effort and expense of a bespoke suit then you may as well start in the right place.

If you have seen a suit in a magazine, book or elsewhere then by all means take it to a tailor. As the old saying goes, a picture paints a thousand words, and so it is much easier to demonstrate what you are after by showing a tailor a picture. Then browse the material samples that the tailor has and discuss the finer details of the suit, including any personalisation. Make sure you ask how long it will take to make as popular tailors will often have long waiting lists for suits.

Finally if all is well then the tailor can measure you up and get started on your suit. Most places will want to see you for at least another fitting when the suit is partially complete, and possibly a third fitting to finish it off. When going for fittings don't be afraid to speak up if you are unhappy with the fit, you are the customer that is paying after all.

Managing your wardrobe and Packing

So hopefully by now you have got some great clothes to fill your wardrobes and drawers with, or are in the process of weeding out what you no longer require. The next step is to think about logically ordering all of these clothes to keep them in the best condition and make getting dressed as quick and easy as possible.

First let's look at what should be hung and what should not:

1.   Suits and shirts should always be hung up, it allows them to retain their natural shape and for shirts stops creasing once ironed. To care for your clothes best get some good quality wooden hangers with broad, rounded shoulders. This helps keep the shoulders of shirts and suits from stretching which can happen with thin hangers. Especially avoid metal wire hangers.

2.   Sweaters should always be kept in drawers. The way wool is knit for sweaters lends them to miss-shaping easily on hangers and can really ruin a sweater's shape. If this happens then rescue it by cold hand washing it then lay flat to dry, reshaping the material to its former shape with your hands.

3.   T shirts can also fall foul of hangers to a lesser extent and should also be kept in drawers or on shelves.

4.   For jeans and trousers storage is generally less of an issue. Suit trousers should be hung, either over a normal hanger, or better still using a trouser hanger which grips to the cuffs of the trouser so that they hang down without naturally without folding. Jeans can quite happily be folded in a drawer, just make sure they are folded flat and don't crease.

When it comes to folding items, take a look at how shop assistants do it next time you are in a shop. It may look difficult, but it's actually rather simple and for T shits and sweaters is the best way to fold for putting items in drawers.

If you regularly wear ties and have a few then it is worth investing in a tie rack; they aren't expensive and are a practical way of storing a number of ties neatly.

Caring for shoes

Hopefully it should be obvious that smart shoes need to be polished regularly in order to keep them at their best and you looking your most stylish. For black shoes it is fairly easy using black polish, but certain lighter coloured shoes can change their colour if care isn't taken. Brown and tan polishes can make brown shoes darker over time, so it is advisable to use a neutral/colourless polish or a leather cream with lighter browns in order to keep them in their original colour.

It is also helpful to use wooden shoe shapers, illustrated below, to keep shoes at their best. These will allow shoes to keep their natural shape which will have been deformed while wearing them.

Suitcase Packing

When packing to go away think carefully about what you really need. We always blame women for being terrible for taking far too many clothes when they pack, but most men are guilty of this too! Try and think ahead about how many days you are going for and then think what you are going to wear for each of those days. For a short trip this shouldn't too difficult and will result in a much less full case.   A case with space is a good case as it means clothes won't be being pressed hard against each other creasing up.

When packing the case always put heavy items such as shoes and toiletry bags at the bottom, and if you have a pull-along case with wheels at one end, put them at that end too. This will stop them dropping through all the clothes, dragging everything out of place. You should also look to put shoes in a bag to avoid getting clothes dirty and pack the shoes with underwear or socks, this will stop them from being squashed out of shape.

Next lay trousers in the case, folding the minimum number of times possible, then T-Shirts, shirt and sweaters. Fill the gaps with socks and underwear. For ties, either lay flat or single folded between layers of soft clothes. Alternatively carefully roll them up and place them in loose gaps (don't force ties into tight gaps where they will crease).

Stylish Luggage

When travelling anywhere it is a shame to ruin a well thought through combination of clothes by then wandering around an airport with a scruffy sports backpack. Instead branch your style into luggage as well and treat yourself to a piece of quality hand luggage. There are plenty of very good leather holdalls small enough to use as hand luggage out there for a reasonable price. The illustration below shows a typical one:

Outro and Acknowledgements

The idea for this book came about when advising a friend what to wear for a date he was going on. He had gone with the failsafe jeans, shirt and shoes option. He looked fine, but was a far cry from projecting the 'wow' factor that he wanted. It was the details that were missing. The shoes were an odd colour of brown and had a clumpy sole. The shirt seemed to drown his otherwise well shaped physique. The recipe was there, but the ingredients were wrong.

He saw the way I looked at him, "What?" he said quizzically, "Well….. here, try this shirt instead" I mimed, handing him something a bit more fitted, freshly pressed with the collar standing up smartly. That was better. "Now, here stick this jacket on too". He protested that it was warm outside that evening, "Hand it into the cloak room when you get there then. This is about first impressions mate, she only needs to see you arrive with it on, after that you can ditch it", "and anyway, it'll take her eyes off those bloody shoes!!" I said winking. He spun around, looking at the sharper version of himself in the mirror. The confidence gave him an extra inch of height immediately. "You should write a book on this stuff" he retorted cheerfully. Maybe he was onto something.

I'd always had an interest in mens' style and often used the internet to find odd tips when needed. I knew that there were plenty of fashion blogs and internet forums in existence, but many simply covered transitory trends, which were out dated the moment they were written. I was a reader of various magazines, but these too were hit and miss, often focussing on selling whichever brand was paying them the most for advertising that month, rather than giving valuable tips to the reader (well they do have to make money somehow!). I thought back to what my friend had said and set about on a course to gather all I could about every detail of different types of menswear and how it all fitted together, creating a reference for real style, rather than passing fads.

This book is the result of that long journey. I hope it will be the stylish friend standing over your shoulder before you leave home, whether you are dressing to go for an interview, the beach or on a hot date, ready to give you helpful, straightforward advice to help you grow that inch of confidence too.

Printed in Great Britain
by Amazon